What does God want from me?

José Leonardo Almanzar Jr.

The first edition was printed in Spanish 2007 by Editorial de las Americas, Corp. Miami, Florida, USA. All rights reserved. Jose L Almanzar

Second Edition 2014 USA

Third Edition 2016 USA

Dedications

To God.

To the ***"wife of my youth"*** (Prov. 5:18-b), of today and forever, my beloved wife Lily. A faithful companion and inspiration.

To my sons Joel and Josh, beautiful gifts from God, I love you with all my heart.

To my parents José and Norma, gone but never forgotten.

To my sisters Ana Palmira and Orietta, clear examples of effort and determination, thank you for all your support.

To All my family.

To my brothers in the faith all around the world.

And to anyone that wishes to embark in the beautiful way of obedience to the will of God, this book is for you.

"I delight to do your will, my God, and your law is within my heart." (Psalm 40:8)

lives practicing what we read to have a good spiritual health.

If we try to interpret every word of the Bible and do an exegesis of everything we read we will never understand the general sense of what God wants to say and thus enter into the frustration that we spoke at the beginning and most likely never finish reading the Bible to the end. That is why we need to read within the context. We will explain that later on this book.

The Bible is a very special book for several reasons, first and foremost is because it is the Book of God that was written while being inspired directly by Him. But there are other reasons that make this a very unique book, for example the fact that it was not written by a single author in one geographical location as nearly all religious books, but as the name implies, Bible means "a set of books" because it is a compilation made by more than 40 authors over a period of more than 1500 years.

Even the characteristics of the authors are so varied that include kings, like Solomon, shepherds, like David, illiterate people, as the Apostle Peter, scholars, as the Apostle Paul and even as a special blessing we have a book included in the canon whose authorship is unknown, the book of "Hebrews".

This symbiosis leads to a variety of literary styles such as **poetry,** as in most of Psalms; **metaphors,** as when the Lord compares a wise man to another that built his house on a rock; **parable**, as the Parable of the sower, where the seed is the word of God and the different terrains are the different types of listeners, and **simile**, as when the Apostle says that Satan is like a roaring lion seeking someone to devour.

Despite this great diversity of authors and literary styles the Bible has an amazing doctrinal uniformity and without any contradictions whatsoever. This is because the styles we have mentioned are not the primary language in which God communicates, but serve as a way to illustrate or emphasize an issue; but 95% of the Scriptures is written in a **literal** way, it means just what it says. In other words, most of the Bible is easy to understand, if you do simply read it in a literal way but, as we will explain in deep in chapter 3, we have to read within a dispensational context. In other words what God say to one generation may not apply to another.

For example in *Luke 9:54-56* ***"When the disciples James and John saw this, they asked, Lord, do you want us to call fire down from heaven to destroy them? But Jesus turned and rebuked them."*** *The disciples were trying to do what was ordered to another generation.* And in *Matthew 5:38* ***"You have heard that it was said, 'Eye for eye, and tooth for tooth', but I tell you, do not resist*** *an evil person. If anyone slaps you on the right cheek, turn to them the other cheek also.*

Again, the Bible is easy to understand, if you do simply read it in a literal way, within its context.

"Every good gift and every perfect gift is from above, coming down from the Father of lights with whom there is no variation or shadow due to change." (James 1:17)

Part I:
The General Will of God

Reading the Bible to discover what God wants from mankind.

"The heavens declare the glory of God; the skies proclaim the work of his hands"

(Psalm 19:1)

Chapter 1

When reading the Scriptures, keep in mind these three suggestions.

First suggestion: **Interpret things literally whenever possible.**

In other words, try to make sense of what you are reading, do not try to find a parabolic or metaphorical interpretation everywhere, as this can lead to confusion. For example, if the Bible says that God made the world in seven days, why do you have to think that the Bible is talking about something figurative and they were not days but millennia or centuries? Does God not have the power to make the world in seven days? In other words, do not try to interpret God unless necessary. Remember *that the Bible was not written for theologians but for the common people.*

When we read in a literal way we begin to understand many things that were confusing because of the myths and misconceptions. You will be surprised with how easy it is to understand the Scriptures when you read them in a simple and literal way. Where it says white it doesn't say pure but just white, do not try to be more spiritual than God.

The error of the Scribes was trying to explain the Scriptures so much, that they even wrote whole books explaining them. This included commandments which weren't necessarily what God wanted but what they interpreted. For example, if one of the commandments say **"Remember the Sabbath day, to keep it holy. *Six days shalt thou labor, and do all thy work: But the seventh day is the Sabbath of the Lord thy God: in it thou shalt not do any work.*"** (Exodus 20:8-10), the interpreters of the law invented that on the Sabbath you could not walk more than a mile but then they also added a trick that if one takes a rest along the way it was permitted to walk another mile as if they were starting again from zero, and so another break and another mile etc. Jesus, by healing on a Saturday, showed that God did not mean what the Scribes said. With "works" God did not mean not to walk or not to do good but to rest. That's the risk we run when we try to interpret God.

Do not interpret what God means when the things He says are clear and need no explanation, please understand that *the Bible was not written for theologians but for the common people*, and that if we understand literally what God is telling us we can obey Him easier. When the Bible uses a rhetorical figure it is to illustrate or emphasize a spiritual truth too difficult to understand. When what is being read does not have literal sense, then and only then start seeking explanations. But before looking in other books, start from the inside out, as many times the meaning is in another passage in the Bible.

Second suggestion: ***If literal has no sense, try to find the meaning in the Bible itself***

If what we are reading does not have a literal sense or it is not clear, do not immediately go to the opinion of others, but seek for another passage in the Bible that talks about the same subject, which perhaps will clarify the meaning without seeking another source. For this there are several methods, but we recommend the following:

Find the meaning within its context

Read what is before and after the text in question. Most of the time this alone solves the problem. Look at an example in *I Corinthians 15: 19*, where the apostle says, **"If in this life only we have hope in Christ, we are of all men most to be pitied."** If we read this isolated text, we can think God is telling us that believing in Christ makes us to be pitied, but that is not it, as the Apostle Paul is speaking of the resurrection and that not only in this life we must hope in Christ but also in the coming life, and this is explained in the preceding and following verses *V16 " For if the dead are not raised, not even Christ has been raised; and if Christ has not been raised, your faith is worthless; you are still in your sins....".* And also in the verses that follow *V20 - 21 "But now Christ has been raised from the dead, the first fruits of those who are asleep. For since by a man came death, by a man also came the resurrection of the dead."*

Find meaning in another passage of the Bible

Another passage may help you to better understand the meaning. For example, in *Matthew 1:25* the writer says about Mary that Joseph *"knew her not until she had given birth to a son."* What does this mean? Is he talking about that they had not met each other? If we look at other passages we will find *Genesis 4: 1*, where it is written *"Now Adam knew Eve his wife, and she conceived and bore Cain ..."* then we understand that '*knew*' means he had sex with his wife. Therefore we can assume that in Matthew's account it becomes clear that Joseph had no relations with Mary until after the birth of Jesus.

Third suggestion: **Recognize the rhetorical figures.**

If what you are reading definitely doesn't make any literal sense, and there are no other passages to check out, try to understand which rhetorical figure the author is using. Many of the concepts that we define as "figures" are explained in other passages such as many of the parables, where we can find many figures the Lord Himself explains as the Parable of the Weeds or the Parable of the Sower, etc. What rhetorical figures can be found in the Scriptures? Here we study the most common.

A. Parable

As its root suggests, the prefix "para" means that something is *comparable to* or of *similar meaning to another thing*. It is the same root used in the word parallel. Typically it is used in literature to describe something that is unknown to known elements. This figure is widely used by politicians to convince listeners of their plans without going into technical details that no one would understand. For example, if you want to explain in the radio what is a "zebra" to a Latin American peasant who has never been to Africa or a zoo, do not start by talking of quadrupeds or mammals they may not understand any of it; but if you tell them it's like a donkey wearing thick striped pajamas or wearing a jailbird outfit, perhaps he will have a better idea since you are using terms that he does know.

Jesus Christ was dealing with people that knew many agricultural concepts, since the geographical areas where he preached relied heavily on climate to survive. For example, in Egypt the weather is so deserted that the sole reason there was a civilization there was thanks to the Nile River. The same applies to the Jordan and the area where Jesus lived. So this is why Jesus uses this style so much, comparing heavenly things with agricultural concepts like "seeding", "fig tree", etc.

B. Hyperbole

Hyperbole is a figure that illustrates the importance of a fact by exaggerating it. For example, in the famous phrase "a picture is worth a thousand words", the number one thousand is not quantifiable but it means many words. In other words, it means that seeing something that is happening avoids a description of the event which uses many words and in such case the thousandth does not have a literal meaning. Here the literal interpretation does not make sense: if so, 999 words would have more validity than an image, which is absurd. Similarly, when you tell someone "a million thanks" you are using a hyperbolic figure of speech (which is the hyperbole) and everyone understands that the phrase is not to be taken literally.

When the Lord says: *"... it is easier for a camel to go through the eye of a needle, than for a rich man to enter the kingdom of God"* (Matthew 19:24) do not try to understand what is the eye of a needle or try to define it as "the hole that was pierced in the walls to give water to a camel without letting him in", or "a sewing needle having such a fine hole that sometimes it is difficult to pass the thread"; here the meaning of the word "needle" does not matter (the plain fact is that it is difficult) just the hyperbolic figure meaning that it is difficult for a person who trusts in his riches to accept God as the supplier of all his needs, so it is difficult for this person to trust God and have the capacity to enter into the kingdom of heaven.

C. Simile

The simile is a literary figure only used to compare the attributes of one thing to another without meaning they are the same (sense of identity) but with the same characteristics. For example, *"Your enemy the devil prowls around like a roaring lion looking for someone to devour."* (I Pet. 5:8), does not mean that Satan is a lion, but it is similar to a hungry lion when it's behind his prey: precise, unmerciful, deftly, angry, strong, etc. A simile is easily identifiable, because it is almost always preceded by words that imply comparison: just as, like, as of, etc.

Therefore, when we see words like these, we do not look for literal interpretation, as it would be distorting the meaning.

Take for example Acts Chapter 2 when Lucas writes about the coming of the Holy Spirit at Pentecost in verses 2 and 3, stating: *"And suddenly there came from heaven a noise like a violent rushing wind, and it filled the whole house where they were sitting. And there appeared to them tongues as of fire distributing themselves, and they rested on each one of them."* (Acts 2: 2-3.)

In these verses we can find 2 similes: the first compares the noise they heard to a rushing mighty wind. It doesn't say that a violent wind filled the house, but a roar filled the house compared to the sound of a rushing mighty wind. For this small mistake many people say the Holy Spirit is like a wind and they think that the presence of the Holy Spirit is manifested in the form of wind, but here it just means a loud sound.

The other simile is when he says "as... fire", he doesn't say they were *tongues of fire* but *tongues as of fire*. The emphasis is in the characteristics of fire not in the tongues. One of the characteristics of "Fire" is what we see in the work of the Holy Spirit as in the case of *Isaiah 6:6-7*, "**Then one of the seraphim flew to me with a burning coal in his hand, which he had taken from the altar with tongs. He touched my mouth with it and said, "Behold, this has touched your lips; and your iniquity is taken away and your sin is forgiven."** Isaiah's lips were touched by a burning coal to purify him and let him stand in the presence of God. Thus the work of the Holy Spirit cleanses us to do the work of God on this earth. Fire purifies, burns impurities and lets the transcendence of God shine on us. The simile then is a comparison used to give more emphasis to a truth.

D. Poetry

This kind of language not only beautifies Biblical literature and gives it the brightness that breaks the monotony of simple facts and regulations, but allows both the writer and the reader to get closer to God to worship him freely. Psalms, Proverbs, the Song of Solomon and other parts of the Scriptures are written in poetic language. This type of literature has a special license to say things that are not allowed in plain language.

For example, to express love to his wife and to compare it with the love of God in a masterful way, as Solomon did in the Song of Solomon, which only can be achieved by using a poetic language, *"May he kiss me with the kisses of his mouth! For your love is better than wine. Your oils have a pleasing fragrance, your name is like purified oil; therefore the maidens love you. Draw me after you and let us run together! The king has brought me into his chambers. We will rejoice in you and be glad; we will extol your love more than wine. Rightly do they love you?"* (Song of Solomon 1: 2-4).

"Heaven and earth will pass away, but my words will not pass away." (Mark 13:31)

Chapter 2

When reading the Scriptures, do not try to be Holier than God.

If we want to do the will of God we should not adapt it to our particular situations and justify our actions as if they were to please God.

There are three types of situations we face daily:

1. Biblical, that is, those where the will of God is clearly expressed in the Scriptures.

2. Unbiblical, those where the opposition of God is clearly expressed in the Bible.

3. Extra-Biblical, situations in which for some special reason God does not issue its opinion in favor or against, but leaves it to our free will with the help of the Holy Spirit.

The extra-biblical situations, like rhetorical figures, are the exception rather than the rule. A common error of believers is to think that God has forsaken all situations to our free will. We often ask ourselves: does God accept this or not? Before consulting the Scriptures. Before doing a conjecture or jump to a conclusion, we should first rule out if it is in fact a Biblical or Unbiblical situation.

In this chapter we will study 4 examples in which we will see clearly that trying to be more spiritual than God is not what He wants. God wants a sincere worship, not an acted one.

The first example: *Aaron and the Golden Calf*

In chapter 32 of Exodus we see Aaron trying to be more spiritual than God Himself, who had said that men could not create any image of what is in heaven, **"You shall not make for yourself an image in the form of anything in heaven above or on the earth beneath or in the waters below."** (Exodus 20: 4). Since the people are desperate because Moses dilates in his meeting with God on the mountain and they demand Aaron to make a calf to worship. Instead of saying, "No, God does not want that" Aaron orders to melt all the gold earrings to make a calf as people demanded and then committed the irreverence of preparing a "feast to the Lord" with the calf. "**When**

Aaron saw this, he built an altar in front of the calf and announced, 'Tomorrow there will be a festival to the LORD.'" (Exodus 32:5)

Of course, God was angry and sent Moses to come down and end the idolatry. *"Then the LORD spoke to Moses, "Go down at once, for your people, whom you brought up from the land of Egypt, have corrupted themselves.*" (Exodus 32: 7)

The Second example: **The Bronze Serpent**

At one time in the desert, the people of Israel got tired of eating the "manna" and they started to speak badly of God and Moses, *"Then they set out from Mount Hor by the way of the Red Sea, to go around the land of Edom; and the people became impatient because of the journey .The people spoke against God and Moses, 'Why have you brought us up out of Egypt to die in the wilderness? For there is no food and no water, and we loathe this miserable bread.'"* (Numbers 21:4-5)

*"The Lord sent fiery serpents among the people and they bit them, so that many people of Israel died. So they came to Moses and said, 'We have sinned, because we have spoken against the Lord and you; intercede with the Lord, that He may remove the serpents from

us.' And Moses interceded for the people. Then the Lord said to Moses, 'Make a fiery serpent, and set it on a standard; and it shall come about, that everyone who is bitten, when he looks at it, he will live. And Moses made a bronze serpent and set it on the standard; and it came about, that if a serpent bit any man, when he looked to the bronze serpent, he lived." (Numbers 21: 6-9)

The act of looking at the serpent on the standard and not be killed by the poison was a symbol of what later Christ would do for us by dying on the cross, as explained by John the Evangelist when he wrote: *"As Moses lifted up the serpent in the wilderness, even so must the Son of Man be lifted up; so that whoever believes will in Him have eternal life."* (John 3: 14-15)

However, the people trying to be holier than God kept the snake as an idol, as if the sculpture itself was the one who had the power instead of God.

Years later, King Hezekiah returned the glory to God by destroying the sculpture of the serpent, which was merely a symbol and not a god as they believed. *"He did right in the sight of the LORD, according to all that his father David had done. He removed the high places and broke down the sacred pillars and cut down the Asherah. He also broke in pieces the bronze serpent that Moses had made, for until those days the sons of Israel burned incense to it; and it was called Nehushtan."* (2nd Kings 18: 3-4)

The third example: **Peter and unholy food**

Let's study the case of the Apostol Peter when he was told to eat food that he considered was unholy:

"On the next day, as they were on their way and approaching the city, Peter went up on the housetop about the sixth hour to pray. But he became hungry and was desiring to eat; but while they were making preparations, he fell into a trance; and he saw the sky opened up, and an object like a great sheet coming down, lowered by four corners to the ground, and there were in it all kinds of four-footed animals and crawling creatures of the earth and birds of the air. A voice came to him, 'Get up, Peter, kill and eat!' But Peter said, 'By no means, Lord, for I have never eaten anything unholy and unclean.' Again a voice came to him a second time, 'What God has cleansed, no longer consider unholy.'" (Acts 10: 9-15)

While is true that God commanded us to abstain from eating certain foods for hygienic or dietary reasons,

"And don't eat pork, since pigs have divided hoofs, but they do not chew their cud. Don't even touch a dead pig!

You can eat any fish that has fins and scales. But there are other creatures that live in the water, and if they do not have fins and scales, you must not eat them. Treat them as unclean." (Deuteronomy 14:8-10), the fact remains that if God sends you to eat something it is because He already cleaned it and saying no, means that you want to be more spiritual than God. When Peter said "Lord no, that's unholy", he was insinuating that he was holier than God.

The fourth example: *Paul persecuting believers in the name of God*

The Apostle Paul later admits he sinned of being more rigorous in the zeal of God that came to persecute believers, *"I myself was convinced that I ought to do many things in opposing the name of Jesus of Nazareth. And I did so in Jerusalem. I not only locked up many of the saints in prison after receiving authority from the chief priests, but when they were put to death I cast my vote against them. And I punished them often in all the synagogues and tried to make them blaspheme, and in raging fury against them I persecuted them even to foreign cities."* (Acts 26:9-11) To the extent that when they stoned the deacon Stephen he gave his vote in favor of the legalists of the time.

These examples teach us how often we like to interpret God and we do not give Him a chance to guide us in His infinite love to a more intimate experience, where what counts is not the dead letter, but the spirit of the law, which on its last expression is love. Let's be simple and sincere in our worship and not pretend to explain to God what He meant by his word.

And God saw everything that he had made, and behold, it was very good. (Gen 1:31)

Chapter 3

When reading the Scriptures, understand that God's plan is progressive and dynamic

"The Dispensational context of what you are reading."

While it is true that God today is the same as He was yesterday, and will be forever, it is nonetheless true that His plan is progressive and dynamic. The Bible shows us how God leads His people as a father would lead his son. *"When I was a child, I talked like a child, I thought like a child, I reasoned like a child. When I became a man, I put the ways of childhood behind me."* (1. Corinthians 13:11)

The Apostle Paul speaks of a change in the way a child behaves or thinks when compared to an adult. Just as it would be unwise to try to teach a one-year old child complicated scientific explanations about why he should wash his hands to avoid getting a disease, so God through a series of regulations or laws instructed His people to help them grow.

Consider a father teaching his child to cross the street at various stages of his life. When the child is one year old, the father says to him: "do not cross the street, if you do, I will punish you." When the child is 7 years old, the father tells him: "first look to both sides and only cross the street when there are no vehicles coming." At 15, the father says nothing or just warns him to cross only when he thinks it's prudent. It is not that the parent has changed, but the child is already becoming a man and maturity allows him to make decisions for himself and the father knows that his son can decide by himself.

The same thing happens in the Scriptures. The law contains a series of ordinances that are hygienic or dietary like not eating meat from certain animals, for example, to make us understand in our childhood what is good for us. It is not necessary for God to speak about trichinosis in pork or the difficulty of our body to break down fats found in that kind of meat. The same applies to the rites of purification: wash your hands, your feet or your body several times, etc.

"Then some Pharisees and scribes came to Jesus from Jerusalem and asked, "Why do your disciples break the tradition of the elders? They do not wash their hands when they eat." 3Jesus replied, "And why do you break the command of God for the sake of your tradition..."" (Mathew 15:1-3)

Jesus Christ explained the laws in the Old Testament when he showed us their correct interpretation in the New Testament. *"You have heard that the ancients were told, 'you shall not commit murder' and 'Whoever commits murder shall be liable to the court.' But I say to you that everyone who is angry with his brother shall be guilty before the court,"* Matthew 5: 21-22.

The law is a schoolmaster, a nanny, to take us by the hand and present us to the true law, the law of freedom in Jesus Christ. *"Before this faith came, we were held in custody under the Law, locked up until faith should be revealed. So the Law became our guardian to lead us to Christ, that we might be justified by faith. Now that faith has come, we are no longer under a guardian...."* Galatians 3:23-25

Also, today we cannot say specifically that God commands us to eat certain types of food. We are in a stage of maturity where God tells us, *"Eat anything that is sold in the meat market without asking questions for conscience' sake"* (1 Corinthians 10:25).

This does not mean, in any way, that God has changed, but God's plan is progressive to help us during our growth until we all reach maturity in Jesus Christ. *"Until we all reach the unity of faith and knowledge of God's Son. God's goal is for us to become mature adults—to be fully grown, measured by the standard of the fullness of Christ."* (Ephesians 4:13)

We know that the original plan of God was for man not to eat meat, but vegetables, *"Then God said, 'I give you every seed-bearing plant on the face of the whole earth and every tree that has fruit with seed in it. They will be yours for food."* Gen 1: 29. *"All things are lawful, but not all things are helpful."* (I Cor. 10:23) Then it is suitable to be vegetarian for health reasons but it is not a dogma of faith.

We cannot understand the scriptures if we do not understand that God has a progressive plan and not all stages are the same: there are at least *7 distinct stages* in the Bible that teach us how God deals with men and what are the rules for all believers during each historical time, until everything is accomplished. Some have called these periods "dispensations".

The original term used by the Bible is "Oikonomia" which could be translated as "stewardship". *"That in the dispensation of the fullness of times he might gather together in one all things in Christ, both which are in heaven, and which are on earth; even in him:"* (Ephesians 1 : 10)

The dispensations are the management of responsibilities God gives human beings over a period of time. As explained in Luke 16:2, the basic idea is that of a butler managing a household.

In each dispensation, God have a different relationship with man and He establishes some rules and a judgement if they are not met. The common mistake of many when reading the Bible is not locating the period in which the events are happening and therefore they confuse the rules for each dispensation. For example, asking the priests to do what they were asked for during the time of Aron with regards to their apparel is similar to Peter questioning God's orders to kill and eat in the example previously mentioned.

In each dispensation we can notice a condition, a failure and a trial. The judgment ends the dispensation and starts another, except for the last one which is the Final Judgment or the White Throne Judgement

Let us briefly discuss the different dispensations in the Scriptures.

The Seven Dispensations: Innocence, Conscience, Civil Government, Promise, Law, Grace and Kingdom.

1. The Innocence (About 30 Years)

God creates the man and puts him in the Garden of Eden with everything he needs and with dominion over the birds in the skies, the fishes in the sea and the animals. It was not possible to steal, because he owned everything; it was not possible to commit adultery, because there was only one woman, etc. The man was completely innocent and pure, because there was no sin. But how does God ensure that man loves him? God tests the man:

The condition: Do not eat *"...of every tree of the garden you may freely eat; but of the tree of the knowledge of good and evil you shall not eat"* (Gen 2: 16-17) The man was not raised as a robot to love and obey its creator without exercising some will, but he was created in the image of God with free will.

The failure: Adam ate *"When the woman saw that the fruit of the tree was good for food and pleasing to the eye, and also desirable for gaining wisdom, she took some and ate it. She also gave some to her husband, who was with her, and he ate it."* (Gen 3: 6) The man fails the test.

The Judgement: Expulsion from the Garden of Eden and physical death *"After he drove the man out, he placed on the east side of the Garden of Eden a cherubim and a flaming sword flashing back and forth to guard the way to the tree of life."* (Gen 3:24)

2. The Conscience *(About 1600 Years)*

After that the man is not innocent anymore because he acquired the knowledge of good and evil; but God now will make him responsible of doing the good rather than the evil. Adam and Eve have two children, Cain and Abel; but Cain becomes jealous of his brother and wants to kill him because God preferred his offerings.

The condition: Do good *"Then the Lord said to Cain, 'Why are you angry? Why is your face downcast? If you do what is right, will you not be accepted? But if you do not do what is right, sin is crouching at your door; it desires to have you, but you must rule over it."* (Gen 4:6-7). Clearly, God is warning Cain to only do good. Cain had not sinned yet and he could be stronger and get over the sin and do the right thing.

The failure: Cain kills Abel *"Now Cain said to his brother Abel, "Let's go out to the field." While they were in the field, Cain attacked his brother Abel and killed him."* Gen 4:8

The Judgement: The Flood *"so the Lord said, 'I will wipe from the face of the earth the human race I have created..."* Gen 6:7 *"But Noah found favor in the eyes of the Lord."* Gen 6:8 *"And after the seven days the floodwaters came on the earth"* Gen 7:10

3. The Civil Government *(About 400 Years)*

Man is unable to let himself be guided by the Spirit of God, neither by his conscience, and he starts a period where God allows him to try and form his own government with some characteristics that separate it from previous periods. For example, with the right to eat other animals or to take the life of another person via the death penalty.

The condition: fill the earth *"Be fruitful and increase in number and fill the earth."* Gen 9:1

    The failure: a sedentary lifestyle. The error was to try and stay in one place instead of filling the earth, and build a tower. *"Then they said, 'Come, let us build ourselves a city, with a tower that reaches to the heavens, so that we may make a name for ourselves; otherwise we will be scattered over the face of the whole earth.'"* Gen 11:4

    Judgement: Different languages. *"'Come, let us go down and confuse their language so they will not understand each other.' So the Lord scattered them from there over all the earth, and they stopped building the city. That is why it was called Babel—because there the Lord confused the language of the whole world. From there the Lord scattered them over the face of the whole earth."* (Gen 11:7-9), which scattered the human race into nations that spoke each language.

4. The Promise. *(About 400 years)*

    The human stubbornness is incredible. God tells them to fill the earth and they want to stay in one place; God then allows them to stay in one place, choose the patriarch Abraham to guide them to the Promised Land, with the sole condition to stay in it, and do you know what happened? They did not stay, they went to Egypt and there came of course the 400 years enslavement.

<u>The condition: stay in Canaan</u> *"The Lord had said to Abram, 'Go from your country, your people and your father's household to the land I will show you. I will make you into a great nation, and I will bless you; I will make your name great, and you will be a blessing. I will bless those who bless you, and whoever curses you I will curse; and all peoples on earth will be blessed through you."* (Gen 12:1-3)

<u>The failure: they went to Egypt</u>. When hunger forced the people of Israel to test their luck in Egypt. *"When the news reached Pharaoh's palace that Joseph's brothers had come, Pharaoh and all his officials were pleased. Pharaoh said to Joseph, 'Tell your brothers, 'Do this: Load your animals and return to the land of Canaan, and bring your father and your families back to me. I will give you the best of the land of Egypt and you can enjoy the fat of the land.'"* (Gen 45: 15-18)

<u>The Judgement: Enslavement.</u> For not complying with the order to stay in the Promised Land, the judgment came rapidly, because after a while a new king took the throne and he was not as kind to Israel as the previous king. He subjected them to slavery and so they spent 400 years of servitude in Egypt. *"Then a new king, to whom Joseph meant nothing, came to power in Egypt. 'Look,' he said to his people, 'the Israelites have become far too numerous for us. Come, we must deal shrewdly with*

them or they will become even more numerous and, if war breaks out, will join our enemies, fight against us and leave the country.' So they put slave masters over them to oppress them with forced labor, and they built Python and Rameses as store cities for Pharaoh." (Exodus 1:8-11)

5. The Law. *(About 1500 years)*

Immediately after the promise have failed, God decides to establish a code of conduct consisting of 613 commandments which we now know as "The Mosaic Law", because God disclosed it through Moses. It is basically contained in the Pentateuch, which are the first five books of the Bible. This long period of the Law ends with the crucifixion of Christ.

The condition: keep my covenant *"Now if you obey me fully and keep my covenant, then out of all nations you will be my treasured possession. Although the whole earth is mine"* Exodus 19:4-5

The failure: Breaking the law. *"Whoever keeps the whole law and yet stumbles at just one point is guilty of breaking all of it." James 2:10*

The error came because of the difficulty of keeping the 600 commandments clearly identified in the first five books of the Bible. If one commandment was violated it was the same as violating all the other commandments and therefore it was impossible to keep the Law. "Why, then, was the law given at all? It was added because of transgressions until the Seed to whom the promise referred had come. The law was given through angels and entrusted to a mediator. A mediator, however, implies more than one party; but God is one. Is the law, therefore, opposed to the promises of God? Absolutely not! For if a law had been given that could impart life, then righteousness would certainly have come by the law.

But Scripture has locked up everything under the control of sin, so that's what was promised, being given through faith in Jesus Christ, might be given to those who believe. ***"Before the coming of this faith, we were held in custody under the law, locked up until the faith that was to come would be revealed. So the law was our guardian until Christ came that we might be justified by faith. Now that this faith has come, we are no longer under a guardian. So in Christ Jesus you are all children of God through faith"*** Galatians 3: 19-26

The Judgement: the crucifixion. It was not paid by any of us but by one that kept all the Law and never sinned and died in our place on an atoning sacrifice, the

Lamb of God who takes away the sin of the world. The judgment was paid by our Lord Jesus Christ on the Cross.

"God made him who had no sin to be sin for us, so that in him we might become the righteousness of God." 2 Corinthians 5:21 *"Christ redeemed us from the curse of the law by becoming a curse for us, for it is written: 'Cursed is everyone who is hung on a pole.'"* Galatians 3: 13

6. The Grace. *(About 2000 Years)*

While the dispensation of the Law was the longest, from Moses to Jesus' death, the dispensation of the Grace is the most significant, because the emphasis is not on what we do but what the Lord did for us.

<u>The condition: to believe in Jesus Christ</u>

"For it is by grace you have been saved, through faith—and this is not from yourselves, it is the gift of God." Ephesians 2:8 *"Not by works, so that no one can boast. For we are God's handiwork, created in Christ Jesus to do good works, which God prepared in advance for us to do."* Ephesians 2: 9-10

<u>The failure: try to be saved by how much work one does.</u> The error is to think that believing in the work of Jesus Christ is too little a condition and we must add

something more for salvation like sanctification or good works. Man wants to justify to himself and not to the word of God, or what God demands. Believing in the work of his Son: this is the only work, an act of faith. *"Then they said: What should we do to put into practice the works of God? Jesus answered and said unto them. This is the work of God, that you believe in that he has sent "*John 6: 28-29

<u>The Judgement: the Great Tribulation</u> after the rapture. *"After that, we who are still alive and are left will be caught up together with them in the clouds to meet the Lord in the air. And so we will be with the Lord forever."* 1 Thessalonians 4:17.

The Lord will descend to the Mount of Olives in his Second Coming as mentioned in Acts 1:11 and he will fight against the army of the Antichrist in the battle of Armageddon in the Megiddo Valley to trap the Beast and the False Prophet and throw them into the lake of fire. *"And I saw the beast, and the kings of the earth, and their armies, gathered together to make war against him that sat on the horse, and against his army. And the beast was taken, and with him the false prophet that wrought miracles before him, with which he deceived them that had received the mark of the beast, and them that worshipped his image. These both were cast alive into a lake of fire burning with brimstone. And the remnant were slain with the sword of him that sat upon the horse, which sword proceeded out of his mouth: and all the fowls were filled with their flesh."* Revelation 19:17-21

7. The Kingdom *(1000 Years)*

Armageddon begins and ends as soon as Jesus Christ overcomes the antichrist. The divine order on earth is established as it had been promised to David: a kingdom. *"When your days are over and you rest with your ancestors, I will raise up your offspring to succeed you, your own flesh and blood, and I will establish his kingdom."* 2 Samuel 7:12

This millennial period is the last period of the Earth as we know it today, before a new kingdom descends from the heavens. The key feature of this period is order and harmony under the leadership of Jesus Christ, who no longer comes as the Lamb of God to pay the price of sin, but as the lion of the tribe of David to rule with a rod of iron. But the latter part of this period is when the thousand years are completed and Satan is released, who returns to deceive the inhabitants of the land and organize them again to fight against the people of God. He will encircle the holy city, and then will come a fire from heaven that will finish Satan definitely, sending him to the lake of fire, where the Beast and the False Prophet have been for the last 1000 years. *"And the devil that deceived them was cast into the lake of fire and brimstone, where the beast and the false prophet are, and shall be tormented day and night for ever and ever."* Revelation 20:10

<u>The condition is to respect the King (Jesus) and persevere as saints until the end.</u> *"You will be hated by everyone on account of my name, but the one who perseveres to the end will be saved."* (Matthew 10:22) Those who came out of the Great Tribulation, to not be marked by the Beast, died beheaded; but now they have risen to reign with the Lord and believers of all previous dispensations including those who were raptured before the tribulation as by grace alone for believing. *"And I saw thrones, and they sat upon them, and judgment was given unto them: and I saw the souls of them that were beheaded for the witness of Jesus, and for the word of God, and which had not worshipped the beast, neither his image, neither had received his mark upon their foreheads, or in their hands; and they lived and reigned with Christ a thousand years."* Revelation 20:4

<u>The failure is to be tricked by Satan after he is released and fight against the forces of God.</u> The nations will join together under the rule of Satan to fight one last time against God.

"And when the thousand years are expired, Satan shall be loosed out of his prison, and shall go out

to deceive the nations which are in the four quarters of the earth, Gog, and Magog, to gather them together to battle: the number of whom is as the sand of the sea. And they went up on the breadth of the earth, and compassed the camp of the saints about, and the beloved city: and fire came down from God out of heaven, and devoured them." Revelations 20:7-9.

<u>The Judgement: the Final Judgement</u> better known as the White Throne Judgement, when God decides to put an end to Satan and everyone who followed him.

"And I saw the dead, small and great, stand before God; and the books were opened: and another book was opened, which is the book of life: and the dead were judged out of those things which were written in the books, according to their works. And the sea gave up the dead which were in it; and death and hell delivered up the dead which were in them: and they were judged every man according to their works. And death and hell were cast into the lake of fire. This is the second death. And whosoever was not found written in the book of life was cast into the lake of fire." Revelations (20: 12-15)

If we read the Bible with this in mind we will not commit the mistake of misinterpreting the text by taking it out of context, as each dispensation has its own requirements. For example, the Law told the congregation not to eat pork; however, by the grace Paul says *"eat anything sold in the meat market without raising questions of conscience."* (1 Corinthians 10:25) This does not mean that we should eat meat, but in no way we should put restrictions where there are none. In this dispensation of grace we are free to choose if we want to eat or not to eat the meat, because we also can live a healthy vegetarian lifestyle *"All things are lawful for me," but not all things are helpful. "All things are lawful for me," but I will not be dominated by anything..."* (First Corinthians 6:12)

The law ordered us to keep the Sabbath while the grace says you are free not to. *"Let no man therefore judge you in meat, or in drink, or in respect of a holyday, or of the new moon, or of the Sabbath days"* (Colossians 2:16)

In the tribulation is said *"the one who endures to the end, he will be saved"* (Mark 13:13) but in the grace says *"... If you declare with your mouth, 'Jesus is Lord,' and believe it in your heart... you will be saved."* (Romans 10: 9) If we place each fragment into its period, there will be no more confusion.

"Listen, my sons, to a father's instruction; pay attention and gain understanding." (Proverbs 4:1)

Part II
The Specific Will of God

Reading the Bible to discover what God wants from me.

Chapter 4

When reading the Scriptures, understand that God's will for us must be in accordance with His plan for all humans

So far we have concentrated on how to read the Bible in a general way by understanding how it is written to avoid misinterpreting. We now understand that the Bible should be studied literally, but taking into consideration its context and all the rhetorical figures used.

This sounds great, *but how do I know specifically what God wants for my life when reading the scriptures?* The first thing to consider is that *God cannot be contradicted, so if God wants something for my life it cannot contradict what He wants for all men.* Taking this as a fact we can already rule out, for example, that God wants me to gamble to feed my family, because in the book it is clear he wants all of us to trust in him not in luck. **"Look at the birds of the air: They do not sow or reap or gather into barns — and yet your Heavenly Father feeds them. Are you not much more valuable than they?"** *(*Matthew 6:26). This is an act of faith since God, not luck, will take care of us. But it does not mean that you don't have to work to get food **"By the sweat of your brow you will eat your food until you return to the ground..."** (Gen 3:19) or as Paul explained, **"For even** *when we were with you, we gave you this rule: "The one who is unwilling to work shall not eat.""* (2 Thessalonians 3:10)

To analyze and understand what God wants for each one us in particular, we will analyze some verses of chapter 12 of the letter of Paul to the Romans.

"Therefore I urge you, brethren, by the mercies of God, to present your bodies a living and holy sacrifice, acceptable to God, which is your spiritual service of worship. And do not be conformed to this world, but be transformed by the renewing of your mind, so that you may prove what the will of God is, that which is good and acceptable and perfect." (Romans 12:1-2)

Chapter 5

When reading the Scriptures, understand that we must have the attitude of genuine consecration.

In the following two chapters we will proceed to do an exegesis of these verses. But the emphasis is in the attitude, not the facts. If you do not get some goals in your consecration but you have the correct attitude that is what God wants.

"Jesus sat down opposite the place where the offerings were put and watched the crowd putting their money into the temple treasury. Many rich people threw in large amounts. But a poor widow came and put in two very small copper coins, worth only a few cents. Calling his disciples to him, Jesus said, "Truly I tell you, this poor widow has put more into the treasury than all the others. They all gave out of their wealth; but she, out of her poverty, put in everything—all she had to live on."

(Mark 12:41-44) Jesus was not watching the amount of the offering but the attitude of the people.

Even when you don't want to do the will of God but you do it anyway, it is better than to promise to do it and then failing to do so. *"It is better not to make a vow than to make one and not fulfill it"*. (Ecclesiastes 5:5)

"What do you think? There was a man who had two sons. He went to the first and said, 'Son, go and work today in the vineyard.' "'I will not,' he answered, but later he changed his mind and went. "Then the father went to the other son and said the same thing. He answered, 'I will, sir,' but he did not go. "Which of the two did what his father wanted?" "The first," they answered. Jesus said to them, "Truly I tell you, the tax collectors and the prostitutes are entering the kingdom of God ahead of you. For John came to you to show you the way of righteousness, and you did not believe him, but the tax collectors and the prostitutes did. And even after you saw this, you did not repent and believe him". (Matthew 21:3 28-32.)

With this in mind let's start the exegesis:

"Therefore I urge you, brethren, by the mercies of God, to present your bodies a living and holy sacrifice, acceptable to God, which is your spiritual service of worship. And do not be conformed to this world, but be transformed by the renewing of your mind, so that you may prove what the will of God is, that which is good and acceptable and perfect." (Romans 12:1-2)

"Therefore", it's an expression that has to do with the context of Romans 11, where the apostle Paul explains in a dramatic way how the chosen people of God is and will remain Israel. Even now, when Israel is in "spiritual blindness" to not recognize the Messiah, it doesn't mean that God has rejected them forever, but only for a while until the number of Gentiles is the right one. Only then, the stage of God will be with Israel at the end of time.

We are branches grafted into the tree of God, but the root remains in Israel. We must not believe we are more than branches, because this is only for a while and we will not always have the grace of God; this is a very special period for us Gentiles who have accepted the Lord and we are living in the time of the dispensation of the grace period. "Therefore", because of this and by understanding how fortunate we are in this time, we should give ourselves to God in an attitude of gratitude.

"I urge you". More than an order, what follows is a plea, a beg, a call to the innermost feelings of all human beings, a reflection to act not only by and for our salvation, but to thank the Lord for saving us. The same apostle in the book of Ephesians specifies that we are not saved by how many good works we did but we are saved to do good works, which is very different. ***"For it is by grace you have been saved, through faith—and this is not from yourselves, it is the gift of God— not by works, so that no one can boast. For we are God's handiwork, created in Christ Jesus to do good works, which God prepared in advance for us to do."*** (Ephesians 2: 8-10).

"Brethren." Paul is not talking to the unbelievers or pagans, he is specifically talking to those who have believed and belong to the Church of God. It is a specific message to those born again by the blood of the Lamb, to those who have received Christ as their savior and now should take line among those who have Christ as their Lord. With "brethren" he refers to the believers in the redemptive work of Jesus Christ.

"By the mercies of God." Not by our works, but because God has mercy on who He wants. We should remember what the Bible says when it tells us about how He loved Jacob but abhorred Esau, or when God liked the offerings of Abel but not the ones from Cain. God had mercy on us and that is why we were not consumed. The apostle Paul tells us to have this in mind when we devote ourselves to God, He chose us by His great mercy not by our works.

"To present." In our language it is difficult to understand the grammatical form of this verb on Greek; but to get an idea let's say that in English we have present, past and future, but in the original language in which it was written, there is a conjugation which is called aorist, or a time that starts at a given moment and then passes to a continuous present that never ends. By paraphrasing Paul, we could say that he meant that we have to present once and forever, and continue to do so daily, our bodies to the Lord.

"Your bodies." Man is a tripartite being in the likeness of its creator, as God is Father, Son and Holy Spirit man is Body Soul and Spirit. We can make an analogy to this similarity noting that the Father is the Soul of God, the Son is the Body of God and the Holy Spirit is the Spirit of God.

Analyzing these three areas of the human being – body, soul and spirit –, we could say (without going into much detail, because it is not the subject of this book) that the **Body** is the part of the human being that makes us aware of what is outside of us and for that it uses the senses; the **Soul** is the part of the human being that makes us aware of what is inside of us and it uses the feelings; and the **Spirit** is the part of the human being that makes us aware of God through the Holy Spirit who dwells in all believers.

Many times the Bible exhorts us to win *Souls* for the Lord or to be filled with the *Spirit*. But in this occasion, Paul urges all believers to present *their bodies*. The body is very selfish and always wants our attention. If I am praying or reading the Bible or studying, the body wants food or rest. The body always wants our attention. Paul exhorts us to present our bodies in the service of God every day.

God, that my eyes see what You want, that my feet go where You want, that my hands touch anything You want, I want to be Your instrument, for your glory Lord: this is my prayer.

"A living, holy sacrifice." The sacrifice that was offered on the altar before Christ was of dead animals, but that was to announce the death of Christ as a lamb without blemishes nor marks, as announced by John the Baptist when he said: "…Look, the Lamb of God, who takes away the sin of the world! (John 1:29) But now Paul wants us to be **living sacrifices** to God, i.e. that we sacrifice by abstaining of some things our bodies want in order to fulfill our mission as collaborators of God's work on earth.

"Acceptable to God." This sacrifice must be a live sacrifice, holy and acceptable to God. With Holy we mean pure, separated from evil; it's not a sacrifice to the body as martyrdom, or sadomasochism which is sin, but a holy sacrifice that is separated from evil and acceptable to God. The obvious question should be: Does God accept what I'm doing? If we answer no, we know that it cannot be God's will for our lives. It may be a sacrifice but not holy or pleasant to God. A sacrifice in vain. ***"Bring your worthless offerings no longer, Incense is an abomination to me. New moon and Sabbath, the calling of assemblies-- I cannot endure iniquity and the solemn assembly. "I hate your new moon festivals and your appointed feasts, they have become a burden to Me; I am weary of bearing them...."*** (Isaiah 1:13)

A holy sacrifice is when you use some time to do something for the Glory of God instead of using that time to satisfy your body or to gain monetary benefit. In other words having some voluntary time for the work of God is acceptable.

"Which is your reasonable spiritual service of worship." The cult or the worship to God is the most reasonable thing to do, after thinking about what he did for us. Worshipping God must also be a form of sincere gratitude, because we always see the hand of the Almighty in our lives. Worshipping Him is the most sublime recognition of God that men can have, it must be something natural for men of God who have always seen His hand everywhere in their lives: that's worship.

In the Old Testament we see many examples about men of God preparing an altar and offering a sacrifice after being favored by God at some time. ***"So Noah came out, together with his sons and his wife and his sons' wives. ... Then Noah built an altar to the Lord and, taking some of all the clean animals and clean birds, he sacrificed burnt offerings on it. The Lord smelled the pleasing aroma..."*** (Gen 8: 18-21)

Chapter 6

When reading the Scriptures, understand that we must have the attitude of separation from this world.

"And do not be conformed to this world." Beware of being molded, or taking the form of this world. The world will always look for ways to mold us with extravagant examples called "fashion". Often these "fashions" make us compromise our faith, so the apostle Paul urges us to not be conformed to this world.

Fear of rejection by society has led many to fall into bad habits or traditions that are not in conformity with Christ. One of the greatest danger faced by young believers is being hard pressed in schools. Classmates that are non-believers make them feel ashamed if they do not like drugs or tattoos like them and teachers ridicule them for believing in God and the **creation** instead of believing in **evolution** for example.

But if we want to know the will of God, then there is no other way and we shouldn't let ourselves be molded by the things of this world. There is a saying that says "In matters of style, swim with the current; in matters of principle, stand like a rock." Thomas Jefferson.

There are trends in the world that we can accept, but in other things we should stay firm, like for example evils like abortion, which people try to justify as a choice or a natural thing to do, being that it is nothing more than the vile murder of a defenseless and innocent creature that began his or her life inside the maternal womb. Quite simply, it is the killing of babies. The calling is clear, "do not be conformed to this world."

"But be transformed". Instead of being molded, we need to be voluntarily transformed, a self-motivated change of attitude. For example, we can be transformed by understanding and keeping the word of God even if we don't feel like it.

The apostle Peter compares the spiritual growth with a staircase of seven steps. ***"Having escaped the corruption in the world caused by evil desires. For this very reason, make every effort to add to your faith goodness; and to goodness, knowledge; and to knowledge, self-control; and to self-control, perseverance; and to perseverance, godliness; and to godliness, mutual affection; and to mutual affection, love."*** (2 Peter 1: 4-7). In addition to faith, after being called to God we must add virtue. Virtue is the attitude toward the good, a renewal of our understanding to be adapted to what God teaches us instead of what we think is good. But on these seven steps of the stair of faith Peter says that we also need knowledge. How can I do what God commands if I don't know what He wants? I should read the bible to add that bit of necessary knowledge. Paul calls for a transformation of 180 degrees to the celestial north, i.e. putting the gaze upward.

"By the renewing of your mind" In this ladder, the first step after salvation by faith is virtue, which is the willingness to do well. Virtue is present in everyone who wants to grow in Christ. The idea is to transform ourselves into the image of Christ. Whatever the Lord says I will do, even if I disagree. The first thing to transform is our thinking, then we can start behaving like Christ. We should aim to walk as the Lord did.

"So that you may prove." A way to ensure that that it is God's will. It's verification. God is pleased when we test Him in the good sense of the word. As in the case of Malachi, when the Lord says ***"'test me in this,' says the Lord Almighty, 'and see if I will not throw open the floodgates of heaven and pour out so much blessing that there will not be room enough to store it.'"*** (Malachi 3:10)

"What the will of God is, that which is good and acceptable and perfect." Only after we devote ourselves to God, presenting our bodies to Him and voluntarily separating ourselves from the trends of this world, we can begin to see what God wants from us, what the will of God is for us. Only then you'll be able to understand what God wants from you. Try it!

Chapter 7

When reading the Scriptures, understand that
We must walk by the Spirit

"But I say, walk by the Spirit, and you will not gratify the desires of the flesh." (Galatians 5: 16)

Whenever we are faced with a situation let's stop thinking about whether or not we should do it, and let's think about what God wants. Our spirit connects us with the Spirit of God and can make us understand what we need. It is not about leaving things to "just happen", but about understanding God's will for us. And only with an attitude of consecration of the **body** and walking by the **spirit** we can expect to hear the voice of God telling us what our **souls** need to hear.

Walking by the Spirit bring us joy and gratitude to God. This is why Peter urges us to fill ourselves with the Spirit, as he says in Ephesians 5:18-20*:* ***"Do not get drunk on wine, which leads to debauchery. Instead, be filled with the Spirit, speaking to one another with psalms, hymns, and songs from the Spirit. Sing and make music from your heart to the Lord, always giving thanks to God the Father for everything, in the name of our Lord Jesus Christ."***

It means that in the same way an intoxicated person will be controlled by alcohol, doing things he wouldn't do in his right mind, like getting in love with a stranger or challenging someone stronger than he, in the spiritual sense someone who is controlled or filled by the Spirit will walk with joy, singing and praising God and giving thanks for everything that happens knowing that God has a purpose.

Let's look at the example of Paul, when he was a prisoner, the apostle said, **"I want you to know, brothers, that what has happened to me has really served to advance the gospel."** (Philippians 1:12)

Our spirit communicates with the Spirit of God and can make us understand what we need. The only way we can expect to hear the voice of God telling us what we need to hear is by understanding God's will for all men and with an attitude of consecration of the body. *"In the same way, the Spirit helps us in our weakness. We do not know what we ought to pray for, but the Spirit himself intercedes for us through wordless groans. And he who searches our hearts knows the mind of the Spirit, because the Spirit intercedes for God's people in accordance with the will of God."* (Romans 8:26-27)

Remember that God speaks, not screams, because speaking louder does not make someone more correct. Only with an attitude of consecration and by letting God speak to us we can tell when a door has been opened or closed, in that way we will begin to understand what God wants from us.

"For everything comes from him and exists by his power and is intended for his glory. All glory to him forever! Amen." (Romans 11:36)

Conclusion

The Bible wasn't written for theologians but for the common people

Many have tried to read the Bible only to stop, thinking it is too difficult to read. By writing this book, we hope to let people know that the Bible was written for everyone, not just for the theologians or seminarians. God wanted everyone to understand Him in a simple and clear way.

In the first part of this book, we explained what God wants for all mankind.

We have given you suggestions when reading the Bible: **Interpret things literally whenever possible**. For the most part, the Bible can be understood in a literal manner. For example, if God says He made the world in seven days… why should we complicate the matter with a bunch of theories! He made the world in seven days, period. **Find meaning in the Bible itself**. If there is a difficult passage, try to find meaning in the Bible itself instead of depending on the opinion of others. **Recognize**

the rhetorical figures. Parable, Hyperbole, Simile or Poetry

Do not try to be more spiritual than God, as Aaron when he made the golden calf and proclaimed a feast to the Lord. Or as Peter, when he tried to explain to God why he shouldn't eat unclean meat even when God told him to kill and eat.

God's plan is progressive. There are at least 7 distinct dispensations in the Scriptures, and each one responded to a specific time period in the Bible.

In the second part of this book, we explained what God wants for each of us individually.

The attitude of consecration, the separation from the things of this world, and to walk by the spirit will help us to be calm and listen to the word of God.

We are confident that God will use this small book to help our brothers in Christ not only to read the Scriptures completely, but also to consecrate more to God so they can live a life fulfilling everything for which we were chosen: to praise the glory of His name.

Epilogue

In this book we are assuming that you are a believer and has accepted Lord Jesus Christ as your Lord and savior. If you haven't done so, you need to know the following:

You cannot have our Lord Jesus Christ as your Lord if you still haven't accepted him as your Savior, ***"For even the Son of Man did not come to be served, but to serve, and to give his life as a ransom for many"*** (Mark 10:45). Jesus came to this world to pay the price that God put to the wages of sin. ***"For the wages of sin is death, but the gift of God is eternal life in Christ Jesus our Lord"*** (Romans 6:23), only by accepting his sacrifice you can be saved. ***"…that if you confess with your mouth, "Jesus is Lord," and believe in your heart that God raised Him from the dead, you will be saved"***. (Romans 10:9) In conclusion, the plan for salvation is simple and has 4 basic steps.

1- Realize that you are a sinner. ***"…for all have sinned and fall short of the glory of God,"*** (Romans 3:23)

2- Recognize that no work can help you be reconciled with God***. "For it is by grace you have been saved, through faith—and this is not from yourselves, it is the gift of God— 9 not by works, so that no one can boast."*** (Ephesians 2:8-9)

3- Recognize that Jesus Christ is the only way to be reconciled with God through his sacrifice in the cross *"Salvation is found in no one else, for there is no other name under heaven given to mankind by which we must be saved."* (Acts 4:12)

4- Repent and receive him in your heart and you'll become a son of God. *"If you declare with your mouth, "Jesus is Lord," and believe in your heart that God raised him from the dead, you will be saved."* (Romans 10:9) and will be a newborn in Christ *"Yet to all who did receive him, to those who believed in his name, he gave the right to become children of God. Children born not of natural descent, nor of human decision or a husband's will, but born of God."* (John 1:12-13)

When you accept him, the Holy Spirit will enter your body and you'll be able to understand the Scriptures *"And you also were included in Christ when you heard the message of truth, the gospel of your salvation. When you believed, you were marked in him with a seal, the promised Holy Spirit"*, (Ephesians 1:13*)* *"... because the veil will be taken away Even to this day when Moses is read, a veil covers their hearts. But whenever anyone turns to the Lord, the veil is taken away. Now the Lord is the Spirit, and where the Spirit of the Lord is, there is freedom"* (2nd Corinthians 3:15-17). *"Because the person without the Spirit does not accept the things that come from the Spirit of God but considers them* *foolishness, and cannot understand them because they are discerned only through the Spirit."* (1st Corinthian 2:14)

This fourth step must be spontaneous and voluntary, not forced and emotional. It is a prayer that comes from your heart to your mouth. I will give you an example, but you shouldn't repeat it as it is, but on your own words. "Father, I admit I am a sinner and I repent, I recognize now that the sacrifice of your son Jesus Christ in the cross was for me and I accept it, I accept you, my Lord Jesus Christ, as my savior, I want to start a new life in your ways. Come to my heart, Holy Spirit and help me understand what God wants from me."

If you have done a prayer of repentance like this one and you believe in Jesus Christ, then according to the Scriptures the Holy Spirit has entered you forever. Now, read the Bible to discover What God wants for you and find a Christian church that allows you to grow, because now you are an infant in Christ and you need the spiritual milk which is the Word of God. *"Like newborn infants, crave pure spiritual milk, so that by it you may grow up in your salvation"*, (1 Peter 2:2

God bless you all.

"When I consider Your heavens, the work of Your fingers, The moon and the stars, which You have ordained; What is man that You take thought of him, And the son of man that You care for him?"

(Psalms 8:3-4)

www.ingramcontent.com/pod-product-compliance
Lightning Source LLC
Chambersburg PA
CBHW041522090426
42737CB00037B/10